SUMMARY OF MANTLES PAST AND PRESENT

What Mantles Are and How They Work

ROBERTS LIARDON

Copyright 2024–Harrison House

All rights reserved. This book is protected by the copyright laws of the United States of America. This book may not be copied or reprinted for commercial gain or profit. The use of short quotations or occasional page copying for personal or group study is permitted and encouraged. Permission will be granted upon request. Unless otherwise indicated, all scripture quotations are taken from the *King James Version* of the Bible. Used by permission. All rights reserved.

All emphasis within Scripture quotations is the author's own. Please note that Harrison House's publishing style capitalizes certain pronouns in Scripture that refer to the Father, Son, and Holy Spirit, and may differ from some publishers' styles. Take note that the name satan and related names are not capitalized. We choose not to acknowledge him, even to the point of violating grammatical rules.

Harrison House P.O. Box 310, Shippensburg, PA 17257-0310

This book and all other Harrison House's books are available at Christian bookstores and distributors worldwide.

For Worldwide Distribution.

Reach us on the Internet: www.harrisonhouse.com.

ISBN 13 TP: 9781667508764

ISBN 13 eBook: 9781667508771

CONTENTS

Introduction	v
1. A Divine Setup	1
2. What is a Mantle?	5
3. Untangling the Threads	9
4. The Operation of Mantles in the New Testament	13
5. Preparation for a Mantle: Pursuit	17
6. The Transfer of the Call	21
7. Qualified to Ask	25
8. The Cost of Saying Yes	29
9. Spiritual Fathers and Sons	33
10. Portrait of a Spiritual Father	37
11. The Vital Role of a Pastor	41
12. Elisha and Elijah: The Unfolding Journey	44
13. A 'Mantle Tour' Through Three Generations	48
14. America's Top Healing Mantle 1st Generation: Maria Woodworth-Etter	52
15. America's Top Healing Mantle 2nd Generation: Aimee Semple McPherson	56
16. America's Top Healing Mantle 3rd Generation: Kathryn Kuhlman	60
17. 'Follow Me, as I Follow Christ'	64
18. Case in Point: William Branham	68
19. Passing on a Mantle: Navigating the Transition	72
20. It's Time!	76
About the Publisher	81

INTRODUCTION

❧

Welcome to "Mantles Past and Present," a comprehensive exploration of the spiritual inheritance that transcends generations, binds the fabric of the Christian faith, and empowers believers to carry out God's sovereign purposes on Earth. This summary distills the profound insights from the complete work, presenting them in a concise and accessible format, tailored to enhance understanding and application for readers from all walks of life.

The concept of spiritual mantles, as revealed through scriptural accounts and historical Church practices, serves as the cornerstone of this book. It delves into the nature and function of mantles as depicted in the Bible, tracing their evolution from the Old Testament's mantle of Elijah, passed to Elisha, to the New Testament's ultimate mantle — the mantle of Christ, given to all believers. This narrative not only bridges the covenantal gap but also illuminates the continuity and expansion of

INTRODUCTION

divine empowerment from generation to generation.

In "Mantles Past and Present," we explore various dimensions of spiritual mantles, including their individual reception, collective impact on the Church, and their critical roles in divine succession. Each chapter of the book builds upon the last, revealing how mantles are not relics of the past but vibrant, active instruments of God's ongoing work in the world.

This summary aims to equip you with the key teachings and revelations from the comprehensive study, allowing you to grasp the significance of mantles in your spiritual journey and in the collective mission of the Church. As you turn these pages, you will discover how to recognize and respect the mantles God has placed on individuals and communities, understand the responsibilities that come with such spiritual gifts, and encourage the proper stewardship and succession of these divine empowerments.

Moreover, this summary addresses the urgent need for the current generation to both reclaim dormant mantles and embrace new ones, as God orchestrates His plans for the end times. Through biblical wisdom, historical examples, and practical guidance, "Mantles Past and Present" invites you to partake in a transformative understanding that bridges divine callings with earthly missions — all woven together by the thread of God's unchanging purpose.

Prepare to be inspired, challenged, and equipped. The journey through "Mantles Past and Present" is not just about learning a concept but about stepping into the flow of God's dynamic power, ready to make a kingdom impact that echoes through eternity. As we embark on this exploratory journey, let us align our hearts and minds to the frequency of Heaven, ready to receive, act, and pass on the sacred mantles bestowed by our Almighty Father.

CHAPTER 1

A DIVINE SETUP

Bible Verse

"For the gifts and the calling of God are irrevocable." – Romans 11:29, NKJV

Introduction

In 1962, Reinhard Bonnke, a freshly graduated student from the Bible School of Wales, experienced what can only be described as a divine setup. During a sightseeing trip in London, he stumbled upon the home of George Jeffreys, a renowned healing evangelist whose teachings he had just studied. This serendipitous encounter would mark the beginning of Bonnke's own remarkable journey in ministry.

Word of Wisdom

"When God gives an order, we're to obey it. If we don't obey, we can abort

the blessing or miracle that He is wanting to bring." Roberts Liardon

Main Theme

This chapter narrates the pivotal encounter between Reinhard Bonnke and George Jeffreys, illustrating how divine appointments can significantly alter the course of one's life and ministry. It emphasizes the continuity of God's work from one generation to another through the laying on of hands and prophetic blessings.

Key Points

- Reinhard Bonnke decided to visit London and unexpectedly found George Jeffreys' residence.
- Bonnke learned about Jeffreys' impactful ministry during his Bible school years, which included notable healing miracles and church planting.
- An inner voice prompted Bonnke to inquire at Jeffreys' house, leading to a direct encounter.
- Despite initial resistance from a housekeeper, Bonnke was allowed inside and met Jeffreys.
- Jeffreys prayed fervently over Bonnke, imparting a spiritual mantle.
- Bonnke learned of Jeffreys' death shortly after their meeting, affirming the significance of their encounter.

SUMMARY OF MANTLES PAST AND PRESENT

Key Themes

- **Divine Timing:** Reinhard's unplanned detour in London led him to the doorstep of George Jeffreys, demonstrating how God orchestrates our steps to align us with His purposes. This event underscores the belief that there are no coincidences in God's kingdom, only divine appointments.
- **Spiritual Heritage and Transfer:** The moment of prayer between Jeffreys and Bonnke symbolizes the transfer of anointing and mantle from one generation to another, highlighting the biblical principle of spiritual succession and impartation.
- **The Power of Obedience to Divine Promptings:** Bonnke's response to the inner voice to explore a mere nameplate exemplifies the importance of sensitivity and obedience to the Holy Spirit's lead, which can result in life-changing divine encounters.
- **Impact of Faithful Witness:** George Jeffreys' life and ministry left a legacy that continued to inspire and activate future generations for the work of the Gospel, illustrating the lasting impact of a life dedicated to God's service.
- **Significance of the Prophetic and Miraculous:** Jeffreys' ministry was marked by extraordinary signs and wonders, reinforcing that the miraculous is a powerful testament to the reality of God's kingdom and serves as a catalyst for revival and faith.

- **Preparation for Ministry:** This encounter was a capstone event for Bonnke, affirming his calling and equipping him for future ministry in Africa. It shows how God prepares and equips His servants in unexpected ways for the tasks He has assigned them.

Conclusion

Reinhard Bonnke's unexpected meeting with George Jeffreys serves as a profound reminder of God's meticulous planning in our lives. This divine setup not only affirmed Bonnke's call to ministry but also equipped him with a spiritual inheritance that would fuel his passion for evangelism. Through this narrative, we see the tangible continuation of God's work across generations, emphasizing that our encounters, especially those divinely arranged, can have eternal implications.

CHAPTER 2

WHAT IS A MANTLE?

Bible Verse
"And Elisha saw it, and he cried out, 'My father, my father, the chariot of Israel and its horsemen!' So he saw him no more. And he took hold of his own clothes and tore them into two pieces. He also took up the mantle of Elijah that had fallen from him..." – 2 Kings 2:12-13, NKJV

Introduction

This chapter delves into the concept of a spiritual mantle, a supernatural endowment from God enabling individuals to fulfill significant kingdom tasks. Using Reinhard Bonnke's experience as a backdrop, it explains the mantle's function, its generational transfer, and its multifaceted nature within the spiritual realm.

Word of Wisdom

"A mantle is a supernatural 'cloak'

that God places on a person of His choosing to accomplish a task of significant importance and that normally flows generationally." Roberts Liardon

Main Theme

The chapter explores the spiritual concept of a mantle, which represents a combination of divine tasks, giftings, and callings transferred from one individual to another, often seen across generations in a spiritual lineage.

Key Points

- A mantle represents a significant spiritual responsibility passed down to fulfill God's plans on earth.
- Reinhard Bonnke received George Jeffreys' mantle not through physical garment but via spiritual transfer.
- The mantle includes various aspects such as callings, giftings, and divine mandates.
- Mantles can sometimes be divided among individuals to carry the full scope of their functions.
- The church-planting aspect of Jeffreys' mantle was believed to have passed corporately to Kensington Temple.

SUMMARY OF MANTLES PAST AND PRESENT

Key Themes

- **Nature and Function of a Mantle:** A mantle is like a spiritual cloak composed of various elements including callings, giftings, and divine mandates, designed to enable the bearer to perform specific tasks vital to God's plan. This supernatural empowerment is crucial for the fulfillment of significant kingdom work.
- **Generational Transfer and Impact:** Spiritual mantles are not only individual but can also be transferred generational, as illustrated by the mantle passing from Elijah to Elisha, and from Jeffreys to Bonnke. This transfer ensures the continuity of God's work across different generations.
- **Multifaceted Components:** Each mantle is woven from multiple 'threads'—from the specific calling of the individual to the anointings required to execute that calling. This complexity allows the mantle to uniquely equip its bearer for the tasks at hand.
- **Division of Mantle Responsibilities:** In some cases, the extensive scope of a mantle's responsibilities may be shared among several individuals or even passed on to a community, as seen with the church-planting mantle transferred to Kensington Temple. This sharing can maximize the mantle's impact and reach.
- **Recognition and Receptivity:** Understanding the nature and operation of mantles is essential for the church to

recognize and support those who carry them. Awareness helps the broader community benefit from the mantle's anointing and contributes to the overall health and growth of the church.

Conclusion

Mantles are not merely historical or biblical artifacts but are vibrant and dynamic elements of God's ongoing interaction with His people. They encapsulate callings, giftings, and divine assignments that are crucial for the advancement of His kingdom. As demonstrated through the lives of Reinhard Bonnke and George Jeffreys, the understanding and acceptance of one's mantle can lead to profound impacts on both the individual and the broader Christian community. This chapter encourages every believer to appreciate the workings of spiritual mantles and to seek God's purpose for their own lives within His grand design.

CHAPTER 3

UNTANGLING THE THREADS

Bible Verse

"For the gifts of the Spirit are given to each one for the profit of all." – 1 Corinthians 12:7, NKJV

Introduction

This chapter clarifies the often-confused terms within the Christian community, particularly among Pentecostal and Charismatic circles, regarding spiritual "mantles," "anointings," "impartations," and "giftings." It seeks to untangle these concepts to ensure they retain their biblical significance and power.

Word of Wisdom

"Different terms like mantles, anointings, impartations, visions, dreams, and encounters can become buzz words without biblical moorings — and in the

process, lose the power of their actual scriptural intent." Roberts Liardon

Main Theme

The focus of this chapter is to delineate the distinct meanings and applications of spiritual terms such as mantle, anointing, and impartation within the Christian faith, emphasizing the importance of precise terminology to maintain their powerful and intended biblical meanings.

Key Points

- Misunderstandings commonly arise in the use of terms like "mantle" and "anointing" within Christian discourse.
- A mantle is a lifetime assignment from Heaven, not merely a spiritual gift or anointing.
- Anointings relate to the Holy Spirit's power given to accomplish specific tasks.
- Impartations involve a transfer of spiritual gifts or empowerment, which differ from mantles.
- Spiritual vocabulary must be used with care to avoid diluting its scriptural and practical significance.

Key Themes

- **Clarification of Spiritual Terms:** The chapter emphasizes the importance of distinguishing between "mantle,"

"anointing," and "impartation," explaining that each has a unique role and significance in a believer's life. Mantles involve a lifetime call, anointings are for specific tasks, and impartations transfer spiritual gifts or empowerments.
- **Misuse of Christian Vocabulary:** The casual or incorrect use of spiritual terms can lead to confusion and diminished impact. It's crucial for believers to understand and use these terms accurately to preserve their powerful scriptural intent and ensure they are applied correctly in life and ministry.
- **The Seriousness of Spiritual Assignments:** Receiving a mantle involves a profound and long-term commitment, unlike the more transient or situational nature of anointings or impartations. This distinction underscores the gravity and permanence associated with mantles.
- **Biblical Examples and Misconceptions:** Through biblical examples and modern misunderstandings, the chapter educates readers on the proper contexts and applications of spiritual terms, aiming to correct popular misconceptions within the church community.
- **The Impact of Accurate Understanding:** Correctly understanding and employing terms like mantle, anointing, and impartation enables believers to more effectively participate in and contribute to the body of Christ,

aligning closer with God's intentions and operations in the world.

Conclusion

"Untangling the Threads" serves as an essential guide for believers to accurately grasp and utilize spiritual terminology, emphasizing the need for precision in language to retain the power and purpose of these divine concepts. Through this understanding, believers are better equipped to recognize and fulfill their roles within God's kingdom, enhancing both personal and communal spiritual growth. This chapter challenges each reader to reflect on and refine their use of spiritual vocabulary, ensuring it aligns with biblical truth and God's calling on their lives.

CHAPTER 4

THE OPERATION OF MANTLES IN THE NEW TESTAMENT

Bible Verse

"But you will receive power when the Holy Spirit has come upon you, and you will be my witnesses in Jerusalem and in all Judea and Samaria, and to the end of the earth." – Acts 1:8, ESV

Introduction

This chapter explores how the concept of mantles, as understood in the Old Testament, translates into the New Testament context. It focuses on how these mantles, transformed by Christ's work on the cross, operate within the body of Christ today.

Word of Wisdom

"Everything from the Old Testament has to come through the Cross before it touches us, and that includes this spiri-

tual transaction of receiving a mantle."
Roberts Liardon

Main Theme

The chapter examines the transformation of Old Testament mantles into New Testament principles of spiritual empowerment through Christ, emphasizing the universal mantle of Christ that every believer carries and the specific mantle assignments that are rare but significant.

Key Points

- New Testament believers all carry the 'mantle of Christ' upon conversion.
- This mantle represents the indwelling of the Holy Spirit shared by all in the Body of Christ.
- Believers are also endowed with power through the Holy Spirit to perform signs and miracles.
- Specific mantle assignments still exist under the New Covenant but are not as common.
- Operating accurately in the spirit realm is crucial for those carrying such mantles.

Key Themes

- **Universal vs. Specific Mantles:** While all Christians receive the general mantle of Christ through faith, signifying the Holy Spirit's indwelling, specific mantles with unique ministerial assignments still exist but are less common in the New Testament era. These specific mantles require a high level of spiritual maturity and alignment with God's will.
- **Transformation through the Cross:** The concept of mantles, like all Old Testament principles, was transformed by Christ's sacrifice. Now, mantles are no longer about individual power but about empowering the Church corporately to fulfill Christ's mission on Earth.
- **Importance of Spiritual Accuracy:** For those called to carry specific mantles, a profound understanding and correct operation within the spiritual realm are required. This ensures that their ministries are effective and aligned with Biblical truth.
- **Dangers of Misuse:** The misuse of spiritual gifts or mantles due to poor understanding or desire for personal glory can lead to ineffective ministries. It is imperative that mantle carriers operate within the scriptural and Holy Spirit's guidelines.
- **Role of Mantles in the Church:** While every believer carries the mantle of Christ, those with specific mantle assignments have the responsibility to equip and build

up the church. Recognizing and supporting these individuals is crucial for the church's overall health and mission.

Conclusion

The operation of mantles in the New Testament shifts from a focus on individual prophets and leaders to the broader empowerment of all believers through the Holy Spirit. While specific mantles with unique roles continue to exist, they are bestowed upon a few to benefit the many, ensuring that the church operates as a unified body under Christ's leadership. This chapter calls for a mature, biblically grounded approach to understanding and operating within the realm of spiritual mantles.

CHAPTER 5

PREPARATION FOR A MANTLE: PURSUIT

Bible Verse

"Elisha then left his oxen and ran after Elijah. 'Let me kiss my father and mother goodbye,' he said, 'and then I will come with you.' 'Go back,' Elijah replied. 'What have I done to you?'" - 1 Kings 19:20, NIV

Introduction

This chapter examines the critical preparatory phase for those destined to carry a mantle, emphasizing the dedication required through the biblical example of Elisha's pursuit of Elijah.

Word of Wisdom

"Folks can know things by the Holy Ghost, but it is the pursuit of what they

know that tells the story." Roberts Liardon

Main Theme

The main theme explores the prerequisites for receiving a mantle, which include a close association with the mantle's current carrier, sustained pursuit, and commitment to the spiritual journey.

Key Points

- Pursuit is essential for anyone called to carry a mantle.
- Association with the mantle carrier intensifies the transfer of spiritual wisdom.
- Staying in the minister's environment is crucial for absorbing their spiritual influence.
- The desire for a mantle must go beyond casual interest to a relentless chase.
- True pursuit requires leaving behind old life and commitments, as Elisha did.

Key Themes

- **Intentional and Sustained Pursuit:** Pursuing a mantle requires more than a passive interest; it demands an intentional and sustained effort that involves personal sacrifices and a shift in life priorities. This pursuit is marked by an unwavering

commitment to follow the mantle carrier closely and absorb their wisdom and spiritual power.
- **Role of Personal Sacrifice in Pursuit:** Elisha's response to Elijah's call illustrates that preparing for a mantle often involves significant personal sacrifices. Elisha not only left his occupation but also used his resources to serve others, demonstrating his commitment to his new spiritual calling.
- **Spiritual Sensitivity and Response:** The initial call to carry a mantle might be sudden and unexpected, as shown by Elijah's casting of his mantle onto Elisha. The recipient's sensitivity to this calling and their immediate response set the stage for their future spiritual journey.
- **Testing Through Persistence:** The journey to carry a mantle is filled with tests of faith and persistence. Elisha's insistence on staying with Elijah until the end, despite being given opportunities to stay behind, exemplifies the determination required to succeed in such a spiritual assignment.
- **Impact of Environmental Influence:** Being in constant association with a spiritual leader allows the prospective mantle carrier to not only learn but also to gradually embody the virtues and anointings of their mentor. This environment is crucial for the transformation from a follower to a leader.

Conclusion

The journey to receiving a spiritual mantle is complex and requires a clear calling, persistent pursuit, and readiness to embrace significant personal change. Through the example of Elisha, we learn that the preparation for a mantle involves both a divine call and a human response characterized by dedication, sacrifice, and the willingness to serve. This pathway is not just about receiving power but about developing the character and depth required to use that power wisely and effectively.

CHAPTER 6

THE TRANSFER OF THE CALL

Bible Verse

"And it came to pass, as they still went on, and talked, that, behold, there appeared a chariot of fire, and horses of fire, and parted them both asunder; and Elijah went up by a whirlwind into heaven. And Elisha saw it, and he cried, My father, my father, the chariot of Israel, and the horsemen thereof." - 2 Kings 2:11-12, KJV

Introduction

This chapter explores the significant moment when the prophetic mantle was transferred from Elijah to Elisha, highlighting the prerequisites and divine orchestration involved in inheriting such a spiritual legacy.

Word of Wisdom

"You find the purpose of God for your life in the place of prayer as you die to self." Roberts Liardon

Main Theme

The chapter delves into the complexities and divine nature of transferring a spiritual call from one generation to another, focusing on the responsibilities and transformations required for those who inherit such a mantle.

Key Points

- Elisha's request for a double portion signifies a desire for increased spiritual responsibility.
- Elijah's parting miracle demonstrates the continuation of God's power through his successor.
- The actual moment of mantle transfer was conditional on Elisha's focused observance.
- Elisha's immediate action upon receiving the mantle confirms his readiness and acceptance.
- The transfer signifies a generational shift in spiritual authority and responsibility.

Key Themes

- **Conditionality of Spiritual Inheritance:** The transfer of Elijah's mantle to Elisha was conditional, emphasizing that spiritual inheritances are not automatic but require certain spiritual conditions to be met. Elisha's ability to witness Elijah's departure was crucial for him to inherit the prophetic mantle.

- **Symbolism of the Mantle:** The mantle represents more than a piece of cloth; it signifies the carrying over of spiritual authority and anointing from one individual to another. This transfer is not just about continuing a legacy but expanding it, as seen in Elisha's request for a double portion of Elijah's spirit.
- **The Cost of Carrying a Mantle:** Inheriting a mantle involves great personal cost, including the dying to personal ambitions and desires. This cost is described as dying to self, where personal plans are surrendered for divine purposes.
- **Impact of Personal Preparation:** The preparation for receiving a mantle is intense and personal. Elisha's journey alongside Elijah prepared him not just in skills and knowledge but in character and spiritual depth, which are essential for carrying such a weighty spiritual responsibility.
- **Focus and Dedication Required:** The necessity for unwavering focus and dedication in the process of receiving a mantle is underscored. Distractions must be managed carefully, with the successor maintaining a clear vision of the spiritual and practical realities involved in their calling.

Conclusion

The chapter thoroughly examines the spiritual dynamics involved in the transfer of a prophetic mantle from Elijah to Elisha, illustrating the profound implications of such a transition. It underscores the necessity of preparedness, the conditionality of inheritance, and the profound commitment required to fulfill a divine assignment. Through Elisha's example, we learn that the continuity of spiritual legacies in the Christian faith hinges not just on God's sovereign will but also on the readiness and focus of those called to carry them forward.

CHAPTER 7

QUALIFIED TO ASK

Bible Verse

"And Elisha saw it, and he cried, My father, my father, the chariot of Israel, and the horsemen thereof. And he saw him no more: and he took hold of his own clothes, and rent them in two pieces." - 2 Kings 2:12 KJV

Introduction

This chapter delves into the qualifications that entitled Elisha to request a double portion of Elijah's spirit, emphasizing the spiritual and relational dynamics necessary for such a significant transfer.

Word of Wisdom

"Elisha's consistent faithfulness to follow Elijah closely and to serve him unconditionally earned the younger man the right to request that double portion when

it came time to transfer the mantle."
Roberts Liardon

Main Theme

The chapter highlights the prerequisites for receiving a profound spiritual inheritance, focusing on Elisha's preparation and the resulting manifestation of his greater anointing.

Key Points

• Elisha demonstrated consistent service and dedication to Elijah, qualifying him to request the double portion.

• The double portion Elisha requested symbolized a continuation and expansion of Elijah's prophetic ministry.

• God honored Elisha's bold request, evidenced by the miracles he performed, which doubled those of Elijah.

• Elisha's qualifications were rooted in spiritual maturity and relational fidelity to his mentor.

• True spiritual succession requires recognition and respect from peers, as seen when the sons of the prophets acknowledged Elisha's new role.

Key Themes

- **Spiritual Preparation and Dedication:** Elisha's right to ask for a

double portion stemmed from his unwavering commitment to Elijah, showcasing that significant spiritual requests require profound personal sacrifice and dedication.
- **Manifestation of the Double Portion:** The fulfillment of Elisha's request is demonstrated through his ministry, where he performed twice as many miracles as Elijah, proving that the double portion was not just a figurative but a literal increase in spiritual power.
- **Divine Approval of Spiritual Succession:** The smooth transition of prophetic authority from Elijah to Elisha illustrates that divine approval is essential for authentic spiritual succession, ensuring continuity and enhancement of the spiritual mission.
- **Recognition by Peers:** The acknowledgment by the sons of the prophets of Elisha's new mantle underscores the importance of peer recognition in confirming a spiritual leader's authenticity and authority.
- **The Role of Spiritual Inheritance in Leadership:** The chapter explores how spiritual inheritance plays a crucial role in religious leadership, requiring not only the recipient's readiness but also a clear endorsement from existing spiritual authorities.

Conclusion

The narrative surrounding Elisha's qualification and his subsequent inheritance of Elijah's mantle provides a compelling framework for understanding spiritual succession. It emphasizes the necessity of preparation, the reality of divine endorsement, and the impact of communal recognition in the effective transfer of spiritual authority. Through Elisha's story, readers are reminded that true spiritual leadership is a combination of personal dedication, divine calling, and communal acceptance.

CHAPTER 8

THE COST OF SAYING YES

Bible Verse

"Then he went up from there to Bethel; and as he was going up the road, some youths came from the city and mocked him, and said to him, 'Go up, you baldhead! Go up, you baldhead!' So he turned around and looked at them, and pronounced a curse on them in the name of the Lord. And two female bears came out of the woods and mauled forty-two of the youths." - 2 Kings 2:23-24 NKJV

Introduction

This chapter explores the immediate challenges and persecutions Elisha faced upon assuming Elijah's mantle, illustrating the inherent costs of accepting a significant spiritual role.

Word of Wisdom

"Persecution and opposition accompany any significant act of obedience to

the Lord. That certainly includes the act of saying yes to the responsibility of assuming a mantle." Roberts Liardon

Main Theme

The focus is on the spiritual and practical challenges that come with accepting a prophetic mantle, emphasizing that significant spiritual responsibilities are often accompanied by trials and opposition.

Key Points

- Elisha faced mockery and persecution shortly after inheriting Elijah's mantle.

- His first miracle demonstrated the transfer of power and authority from Elijah.

- Elisha's response to mockery highlights the serious consequences of disrespecting God's anointed.

- Opposition is a common experience for those who take up God's assignments.

- True obedience involves enduring persecution and continuing God's work.

- Elisha's ministry began with challenges but also immediate validation of his new role through miracles.

Key Themes

- **Immediate Challenges Post-Inheritance:** Right after receiving Elijah's mantle, Elisha encountered severe mockery from youths, an incident that underscores the immediate challenges and spiritual warfare faced when stepping into a new divine role.
- **Spiritual Authority and Public Validation:** Elisha's first act of parting the Jordan with Elijah's mantle not only confirms the transfer of spiritual power but also serves as public validation of his prophetic authority, crucial for establishing his leadership.
- **Persecution as a Consequence of Obedience:** The mockery from the youths and the harsh consequences they faced illustrate that significant spiritual responsibilities are fraught with trials, often manifesting as persecution or direct opposition.
- **The Role of Miracles in Prophetic Ministry:** Elisha's ability to perform miracles similar to Elijah's not only affirms his rightful succession but also emphasizes the continuity of God's work across different generations of prophets.
- **Endurance and Faithfulness in Ministry:** Elisha's experiences highlight the necessity for God's servants to remain steadfast and faithful, even when faced with ridicule or threats, as true obedience transcends personal comfort and safety.

Conclusion

Elisha's early experiences as Elijah's successor teach that saying yes to a divine call is not merely a moment of acceptance but a commitment to face and overcome the spiritual and physical challenges that accompany such roles. His journey emphasizes the cost of spiritual leadership, marked by opposition but also by divine empowerment to continue the work set forth by his predecessors. Through this narrative, believers are reminded of the importance of steadfastness and the inevitability of challenges in fulfilling God's calling.

CHAPTER 9

SPIRITUAL FATHERS AND SONS

Bible Verse

"And it came to pass, as they still went on, and talked, that, behold, there appeared a chariot of fire, and horses of fire, and parted them both asunder; and Elijah went up by a whirlwind into heaven. And Elisha saw it, and he cried, My father, my father, the chariot of Israel, and the horsemen thereof." - 2 Kings 2:11-12 NKJV

Introduction

This chapter delves into the profound spiritual relationship between Elijah and Elisha, emphasizing the father-son dynamic that transcends traditional mentorship, shaping the foundation for the transfer of a prophetic mantle.

Word of Wisdom

"People need more than a life coach.

They need a guiding influence who is stronger and deeper in their lives than a mentor. People need a spiritual parent."
Roberts Liardon

Main Theme

The core of this chapter explores the essential difference between mere mentorship and spiritual parenting, stressing the depth, commitment, and personal involvement required in true spiritual father-son relationships within the faith.

Key Points

• Elisha's reaction to Elijah's ascent to heaven reveals the depth of their bond, highlighting a father-son rather than a mentor-mentee relationship.

• Spiritual parenting involves more than guidance; it includes correction and deep personal investment.

• The real-life influence of a spiritual parent is profound and necessary for handling spiritual responsibilities and mantles.

• Spiritual parents provide not just instruction but also correction, preparing their spiritual children for their future roles.

• The relationship between Elijah and Elisha serves as a model of biblical spiritual parenting.

Key Themes

- **Deep Emotional and Spiritual Connection:** The moment of Elijah's departure highlights the intense emotional and spiritual bond between Elijah and Elisha, demonstrating that spiritual parenting encompasses deep relational ties and a shared life journey, far exceeding the scope of typical mentorship.
- **Role of Correction and Guidance:** Spiritual parents are deeply involved in shaping the character and spiritual maturity of their children, providing not just guidance but also necessary correction, which is essential for growth and preparation for future responsibilities.
- **Transfer of Mantle and Responsibility:** The transition of Elijah's mantle to Elisha underscores the importance of spiritual readiness and character development, which were cultivated through their father-son relationship, preparing Elisha to step into his calling effectively.
- **Importance of Recognizing Spiritual Parenthood:** Recognizing and embracing spiritual parenthood is crucial for receiving and carrying on a mantle. This relationship is characterized by mutual respect, deep personal involvement, and the transmission of spiritual wisdom and authority.
- **Impact of Spiritual Parenthood on Legacy and Ministry:** The legacy of spiritual fathers and mothers significantly

impacts the ministry and spiritual authority of the next generation, ensuring that mantles are passed on with the requisite wisdom and character to use them wisely.

Conclusion

The dynamic between Elijah and Elisha exemplifies the profound impact of spiritual fatherhood on personal development and spiritual inheritance. This relationship goes beyond simple mentorship by embedding a deeper, more holistic approach to spiritual growth and readiness for leadership, emphasizing the necessity of character development over mere skill or knowledge acquisition. Through their interactions, we see the biblical blueprint for spiritual parenting, which ensures the successful transfer of spiritual mantles and the continuation of God's work through successive generations.

CHAPTER 10

PORTRAIT OF A SPIRITUAL FATHER

Bible Verse

"And it came to pass, as they still went on, and talked, that, behold, there appeared a chariot of fire, and horses of fire, and parted them both asunder; and Elijah went up by a whirlwind into heaven." - 2 Kings 2:11

Introduction

This chapter explores the profound influence of a true spiritual father through the author's personal relationship with Dr. Lester Sumrall. It discusses the critical role of spiritual fathers in shaping character and self-governance beyond mere ministerial success.

Word of Wisdom

"That's what true spiritual fathers and mothers do. They go to work on the character of their spiritual children,

which is going to take more time than developing their giftings." Roberts Liardon

Main Theme

The chapter delves into the essential qualities of a spiritual father, exemplified by Dr. Lester Sumrall, focusing on character building and personal involvement rather than just imparting skills or anointing.

Key Points

• Dr. Sumrall exemplified the role of a spiritual father through deep personal involvement and character building.

• True spiritual parenting involves correction, not just agreement and praise.

• Spiritual fathers invest significant time into the personal and spiritual growth of their children.

• The relationship provided critical support during the author's personal crises and ministerial doubts.

• Spiritual fathers see beyond faults and focus on long-term spiritual health and ministry success.

Key Themes

- **Investment Beyond Ministry Skills:** A true spiritual father like Dr. Sumrall

focuses on developing character and self-governance in his spiritual children, which is more challenging and time-consuming than teaching them to flow with the anointing or perform miracles.
- **Correction and Guidance:** Effective spiritual fathers provide not only guidance but also necessary correction. They are committed to the truth, even when it involves confronting uncomfortable issues, which is crucial for genuine spiritual growth and resilience.
- **Long-Term Commitment and Personal Sacrifice:** The role of a spiritual father is marked by a willingness to make personal sacrifices and commit time to nurture and recover those who are spiritually wounded, guiding them back to their calling.
- **Impact on Personal Crisis:** During personal crises, a spiritual father provides not only emotional support but also spiritual direction, helping to navigate through doubts and pain, as Dr. Sumrall did for the author during a critical period of disillusionment with ministry.
- **Legacy of Spiritual Fatherhood:** The true measure of a spiritual father's impact is seen in the continued faith and ministry effectiveness of his spiritual children. Their ongoing success and adherence to spiritual truths affirm the value and effectiveness of his mentorship.

Conclusion

Dr. Lester Sumrall's life and ministry provide a compelling model of spiritual fatherhood, demonstrating the profound impact a spiritual father can have on an individual's personal and ministerial development. Through self-sacrifice, dedicated teaching, and personal involvement, spiritual fathers like Dr. Sumrall shape the character and destinies of their spiritual children, ensuring that their spiritual and ministerial legacies endure through successive generations. This chapter underscores the indispensable role of spiritual fathers in fostering deep, enduring spiritual growth and preparedness for ministry.

CHAPTER 11

THE VITAL ROLE OF A PASTOR

Bible Verse

"Obey your leaders and submit to them, for they are keeping watch over your souls, as those who will have to give an account. Let them do this with joy and not with groaning, for that would be of no advantage to you." - Hebrews 13:17

Introduction

This chapter explores the essential role of pastors in providing guidance, correction, and spiritual stability. It highlights the personal experiences of the author with his pastor, Billy Joe Daugherty, emphasizing the need for pastoral oversight even among those in ministry.

Word of Wisdom

"God intended that every person be submitted to a pastor as a stabilizing force in his or her life." Roberts Liardon

. . .

Main Theme

The chapter underscores the necessity of having a pastor who can offer correction and guidance to ensure that individuals fulfill their divine purposes without stumbling.

Key Points

• Every minister, regardless of their role, needs the stabilizing influence of a pastor.

• Pastors are not inferior to other fivefold ministry offices; they play a unique and critical role.

• Pastoral correction is an act of love meant to remove hindrances in a believer's life.

• Accepting pastoral correction can be challenging but is essential for spiritual growth.

• The relationship with a pastor is a lifelong commitment to spiritual accountability and growth.

Key Themes

- **Essential Pastoral Role:** Pastors provide more than spiritual oversight; they engage deeply with individuals to correct and direct according to God's will, helping prevent minor issues from becoming major stumbling blocks in fulfilling God's call.
- **Correction as an Expression of Love:** True pastoral care involves stepping into personal areas that may feel private to

address issues crucial for spiritual health, done not to embarrass but to ensure readiness and purity in ministry.
- **Resistance to Correction:** Initially, correction may stir feelings of offense or disrespect, but recognizing it as a necessary act of love is crucial for anyone in ministry to progress and mature spiritually.
- **Pastoral Guidance in Ministry:** Pastors help refine ministers' approaches to sensitive topics, advising on semantics and presentation to enhance the effectiveness and reception of the preached word.
- **Long-Term Impact of Pastoral Relationships:** A lifelong pastoral relationship provides continuous spiritual oversight and correction, which is vital for enduring in ministry and avoiding spiritual pitfalls.

Conclusion

Pastors play an indispensable role in the lives of all believers, including ministers. Their guidance and correction are foundational to spiritual stability and effectiveness in ministry. This chapter calls for a renewed appreciation for the pastoral office and encourages ministers to embrace pastoral oversight as a divine provision for their spiritual well-being and success in ministry.

CHAPTER 12

ELISHA AND ELIJAH: THE UNFOLDING JOURNEY

Bible Verse

"Elisha then picked up Elijah's cloak, which had fallen from him, and went back and stood on the bank of the Jordan. He took the cloak that had fallen from Elijah and struck the water with it. 'Where now is the Lord, the God of Elijah?' he asked. When he struck the water, it divided to the right and to the left, and he crossed over." - 2 Kings 2:13-14

Introduction

This chapter explores the profound journey of Elijah and Elisha, focusing on the spiritual significance of their travels through Gilgal, Bethel, Jericho, and the Jordan River. Each location marks crucial spiritual lessons and growth necessary for Elisha before inheriting Elijah's mantle.

SUMMARY OF MANTLES PAST AND PRESENT

Word of Wisdom

"There are milestones in God concerning one's dedication, consecration, and the dealing with one's flesh that must be reached over a period of time in order to be trusted with great power and anointing." Roberts Liardon

Main Theme

The passage through Gilgal, Bethel, Jericho, and the Jordan River symbolizes the necessary stages of spiritual preparation and growth for those who are to receive and carry on a spiritual mantle.

Key Points

• Gilgal symbolizes the cutting away of the flesh and selfish ambitions, essential for spiritual readiness.

• Bethel represents learning and walking in God's ways, crucial for understanding divine principles.

• Jericho reflects the constant spiritual warfare associated with carrying a mantle, highlighting the battle against principalities.

• The Jordan River is where the full operation of the anointing is demonstrated and learned.

• Each location's significance is deeply rooted in biblical history and spiritual symbolism.

- The journey of Elijah and Elisha serves as a blueprint for the transfer of spiritual authority and mantle.

Key Themes

- **Preparation at Gilgal:** At Gilgal, the spiritual journey begins with a covenant to rid oneself of the flesh, symbolizing the initial steps of purification and dedication necessary for those destined to carry a mantle.
- **Instruction at Bethel:** In Bethel, the house of God, a spiritual son or daughter learns directly from their mentor about divine operations and the expectations of covenant, which are foundational for handling spiritual responsibilities.
- **Warfare at Jericho:** The experience at Jericho teaches about the intense and continuous spiritual warfare that mantle carriers face, preparing them for the battles they will encounter as they step into their calling.
- **Anointing at the Jordan River:** The Jordan represents the culmination of spiritual training, where the anointing is fully transferred and the spiritual son or daughter learns to operate in the power that was characteristic of their mentor.
- **Overall Journey:** The entire journey from Gilgal to the Jordan River encapsulates the necessary spiritual growth and battles that prepare a spiritual successor to effectively take up their

mentor's mantle without falling into the pitfalls that previously ensnared others.

Conclusion

The chapter concludes by emphasizing the importance of a communal mindset among prophets, where unity and a shared sense of limitless possibilities enable them to thrive and effect change within the Body of Christ. It also highlights the need for ongoing personal growth, openness to the Spirit, and commitment to fostering a strong, supportive prophetic community.

CHAPTER 13

A 'MANTLE TOUR' THROUGH THREE GENERATIONS

Bible Verse

"And these signs shall follow them that believe; In my name shall they cast out devils; they shall speak with new tongues; They shall take up serpents; and if they drink any deadly thing, it shall not hurt them; they shall lay hands on the sick, and they shall recover." - Mark 16:17-18

Introduction

This chapter explores the transmission of a significant healing mantle through three generations of influential American female evangelists: Maria Woodworth-Etter, Aimee Semple McPherson, and Kathryn Kuhlman. Each of these women played a pivotal role in shaping the national consciousness of healing ministries in America.

Word of Wisdom

"When God wants a certain aspect of

SUMMARY OF MANTLES PAST AND PRESENT

His kindness and His miracle-working power to be demonstrated considerably in the eyes of a nation, He will highlight a person with that gifting." Roberts Liardon

Main Theme

The chapter outlines how a divine healing mantle was passed down through three generations, each marked by significant spiritual impact and similar challenges, revealing the continuous struggle against spiritual opposition but also the profound effect of God's power in their ministries.

Key Points

• Maria Woodworth-Etter, Aimee Semple McPherson, and Kathryn Kuhlman each carried a national healing mantle.

• All three faced significant personal and public challenges, including marital issues and health problems.

• They were initially celebrated by the public and the press but later faced intense scrutiny and opposition.

• Their ministries were marked by notable signs, wonders, and a distinct choice of wearing white during services.

- Each woman's ministry contributed uniquely to the fabric of American evangelicalism and its perception of healing.

Key Themes

- **Historical and Spiritual Significance:** The ministries of Woodworth-Etter, McPherson, and Kuhlman are not just historical footnotes but pivotal moments in the spiritual narrative of America, demonstrating the resilience and power of a divine mantle across different societal epochs.
- **Patterns of Opposition and Victory:** Each of these women experienced a pattern of spiritual warfare manifesting in personal attacks, health issues, and public persecution, underscoring the enemy's consistent strategy to undermine the healing mantle.
- **Symbolic Use of Color and Ritual:** The choice of white attire by each woman symbolized purity and holiness, reflecting their commitment to living out their call in godliness amidst public and private battles.
- **Impact on National Consciousness:** Through their ministries, the concept of divine healing remained a vital part of America's religious landscape, influencing both the church and secular society's understanding of spiritual phenomena.
- **Legacy and Continuation:** Despite their personal struggles, the legacies of these women have inspired subsequent

generations to pursue healing ministries, illustrating the mantle's durability and the importance of spiritual succession.

Conclusion

The journey of the great American healing mantle through these three iconic figures not only illustrates the profound impact of divine anointing but also highlights the relentless opposition they faced. Their stories teach us about the power of resilience, the reality of spiritual warfare, and the enduring grace of God that operates through chosen vessels across generations.

CHAPTER 14

AMERICA'S TOP HEALING MANTLE 1ST GENERATION: MARIA WOODWORTH-ETTER

Bible Verse

"And these signs shall follow them that believe; they shall lay hands on the sick, and they shall recover." - Mark 16:18

Introduction

This chapter delves into the life and ministry of Maria Woodworth-Etter, the first carrier of America's significant healing mantle. It highlights her pioneering role in the Pentecostal movement and her profound impact on divine healing practices in the United States.

Word of Wisdom

"The Lord was visiting them in great mercy and power, and there was great victory coming." Roberts Liardon

Main Theme

Maria Woodworth-Etter's ministry laid the foundational work for the Pentecostal movement in America, characterized by miraculous healings, persistent opposition, and her groundbreaking role as a female preacher in a male-dominated society.

Key Points

• Maria Woodworth-Etter played a crucial role in pioneering the Pentecostal movement in America.

• She experienced significant personal and societal opposition throughout her ministry.

• Her ministry was marked by miraculous healings and speaking in tongues before the Azusa Street Revival.

• Maria faced numerous personal tragedies, including the loss of her children and marital difficulties.

• Despite opposition, she persisted in her calling, significantly impacting the spiritual landscape of her time.

Key Themes

- **Pioneering Female Ministry:** Maria Woodworth-Etter broke societal norms by preaching and leading in a predominantly male religious society, setting a precedent for female ministers in America. Her ministry was characterized by divine healings and the manifestation of spiritual gifts, which were revolutionary at her time.

- **Spiritual Warfare and Opposition:** Maria faced relentless challenges both from within her personal life, including her health and marital issues, and externally from societal skepticism and legal troubles. Her perseverance showcased the typical spiritual warfare associated with carrying a significant mantle.
- **Impact on National Consciousness:** Her ministries influenced the national perception of healing and Pentecostal practices, embedding the importance of spiritual gifts and divine healing in American religious culture. Her legacy paved the way for future generations of healing ministries.
- **The Cost of Spiritual Leadership:** Maria's life exemplifies the personal sacrifices and hardships endured by leaders carrying a divine mantle. Her experiences illustrate the isolation and misunderstanding often faced by pioneering spiritual leaders.
- **Legacy of Faith and Resilience:** Despite numerous setbacks, Maria's steadfast faith and resilience under pressure helped forge a path for future spiritual movements and left a lasting imprint on Christian ministry, illustrating the power of unwavering faith in overcoming life's adversities.

Conclusion

Maria Woodworth-Etter's ministry not only pioneered the Pentecostal movement and set the stage for subsequent generations of healing ministries in America but also demonstrated the profound impact of divine empowerment in overcoming personal and societal challenges. Her story is a testament to the enduring power of faith and the transformative impact of spiritual obedience.

CHAPTER 15

AMERICA'S TOP HEALING MANTLE 2ND GENERATION: AIMEE SEMPLE MCPHERSON

Bible Verse

"Truly, truly, I say to you, whoever believes in me will also do the works that I do; and greater works than these will he do, because I am going to the Father." - John 14:12

Introduction

This chapter explores the dynamic ministry of Aimee Semple McPherson, a seminal figure in the Pentecostal movement and the second generation carrier of America's great healing mantle. It details her revolutionary approach to ministry, marked by significant healings and challenges.

Word of Wisdom

"When I get to the border, they'll lift the quarantine!" - Aimee Semple McPherson

Main Theme

Aimee Semple McPherson's ministry was characterized by her charismatic leadership, innovative evangelistic techniques, and a profound healing ministry that mirrored and expanded upon the works of her predecessor, Maria Woodworth-Etter.

Key Points

• Aimee Semple McPherson was a pioneering leader who brought Pentecostalism into the mainstream in early 20th-century America.

• Her ministry faced significant opposition but was marked by miraculous healings and expansive growth.

• Aimee was known for her theatrical sermons which made her a religious celebrity.

• She founded the Foursquare Church, a major Pentecostal denomination that continues to thrive.

• Aimee's personal life was fraught with challenges, including multiple marriages and a high-profile kidnapping.

Key Themes

- **Healing and Pentecostal Advocacy:**
  Aimee brought Pentecostal beliefs to the forefront of American Christianity, advocating for the power of the Holy Spirit in everyday Christian life and integrating

miraculous healings as a regular part of her ministry.
- **Media and Cultural Influence:** She utilized media, including radio and staged sermons, to reach a wider audience, becoming one of the first to blend technology with evangelism effectively, which significantly extended her influence beyond traditional church settings.
- **Personal Struggles and Public Ministry:** Despite personal tragedies and scandals, such as her controversial kidnappings and tumultuous marriages, Aimee's ministry continued to grow, showing her resilience and the public's reception of her spiritual message.
- **Mentorship and Legacy:** Aimee served as a spiritual mentor to many and left behind a legacy through the Foursquare Church, which emphasized evangelical outreach and Pentecostal practices, ensuring her teachings lived beyond her.
- **Challenges of Female Leadership:** As a female religious leader in a predominantly male-dominated sphere, Aimee faced and overcame significant societal barriers, paving the way for future generations of women in ministry.

Conclusion

Aimee Semple McPherson's ministry reshaped American Pentecostalism and set new standards for church leadership and evangelical outreach. Her life's work, marked by both divine empowerment and human vulnerability, left an indelible mark on

SUMMARY OF MANTLES PAST AND PRESENT

the Christian faith and remains a powerful testament to the capacity for personal transformation and societal impact through faith.

CHAPTER 16

AMERICA'S TOP HEALING MANTLE 3RD GENERATION: KATHRYN KUHLMAN

Bible Verse

"Heal the sick, raise the dead, cleanse those who have leprosy, drive out demons. Freely you have received; freely give." - Matthew 10:8

Introduction

This chapter delves into the life and ministry of Kathryn Kuhlman, a pivotal figure in the Pentecostal movement and the third generation carrier of a profound healing mantle. It traces her journey from personal struggles to becoming a renowned minister known for her miraculous healing services.

Word of Wisdom

"Before I die, I hope someone can say that about me because I helped them." - Kathryn Kuhlman

SUMMARY OF MANTLES PAST AND PRESENT

Main Theme

The chapter captures Kathryn Kuhlman's transformative impact on Christian ministry, emphasizing her unique role in the continuation of a powerful healing legacy, her personal challenges, and her ultimate success in overcoming them to inspire millions.

Key Points

• Kathryn Kuhlman's ministry was marked by dramatic healing services where many experienced miraculous recoveries.

• She faced significant personal and professional challenges but remained steadfast in her faith and commitment to her calling.

• Kuhlman's influence extended through radio and television, broadening her reach and impact.

• Her personal life was fraught with hardship, including a troubled marriage that profoundly affected her ministry.

• Despite setbacks, Kathryn's faith and ministerial practices led to a revival of Pentecostal healing ministries in America.

• She left behind a legacy of faith, highlighted by her dedication to serving God and humanity through her spiritual gifts.

Key Themes

- **Transformation Through Trials:** Kathryn's journey was shaped by personal missteps and societal challenges, yet these obstacles set the stage for her profound spiritual impact. Her story illustrates the transformative power of redemption and perseverance in faith.
- **Healing as a Ministry:** Kathryn's healing services were not just events but expressions of deep faith in the power of God. She demonstrated that divine healing is an integral part of Christian ministry, emphasizing its biblical foundation and transformative potential.
- **Media and Ministry:** Utilizing media effectively, Kathryn expanded her outreach, showing future generations of ministers the power of media in spreading the gospel and engaging broader audiences with the message of Christ's healing power.
- **Legacy of Empowerment:** By overcoming significant personal and societal barriers, Kathryn empowered many, especially women in ministry, showing that spiritual gifts and callings are not confined by gender or personal history.
- **Endurance and Impact:** Despite intense scrutiny and criticism, Kathryn maintained her ministerial focus, which allowed her to leave a lasting impact not only on individuals she ministered to directly but also on the global church community.

Conclusion

Kathryn Kuhlman's life was a testament to the resilience and power of faith. Her spiritual journey was marked by both adversity and triumph, illustrating the profound impact one individual can have when fully committed to God's call. Her legacy continues to inspire and influence the Christian faith, demonstrating that the gifts of the Spirit are timeless and vital to the body of Christ.

CHAPTER 17

'FOLLOW ME, AS I FOLLOW CHRIST'

Bible Verse

"Follow my example, as I follow the example of Christ." - 1 Corinthians 11:1

Introduction

This chapter emphasizes the importance of discipleship in the Christian life, specifically the dynamics of following a leader who is aligned with Christ. It discusses the responsibilities and discernments required when choosing whom to emulate in the spiritual journey.

Word of Wisdom

"You have to know how to follow someone as that person follows the Lord."
Roberts Liardon

Main Theme

The central theme revolves around the biblical principle of discipleship, demonstrating through scriptural and contemporary examples how Christians can effectively follow spiritual leaders who themselves are followers of Christ, thereby avoiding pitfalls while inheriting spiritual legacies.

Key Points

- Christian discipleship involves emulating leaders who exemplify Christ-like behavior.

- It is crucial to discern and follow leaders who successfully navigate their spiritual journey to the end.

- Disciples must be aware of the potential pitfalls that leaders can fall into to avoid following in those same errors.

- The legacy of a mantle, such as the healing mantle, requires understanding previous generational battles and victories.

- Understanding and avoiding the errors of past mantle carriers is crucial for those aspiring to carry on their legacies.

Key Themes

- **Role of Mentorship in Spiritual Growth:** Choosing the right spiritual mentors is vital as they significantly influence one's spiritual development. Followers must discern and emulate leaders

who genuinely follow Christ, ensuring their teachings and actions align with biblical truths.
- **Learning from Past Generations:** By studying the lives of previous spiritual leaders, current and future leaders can learn to navigate their paths without repeating historical mistakes, particularly in the areas of doctrine and personal conduct.
- **The Importance of Discernment in Leadership:** Followers must exercise discernment in leadership, recognizing when a leader deviates from biblical truth and thus when to discontinue following their guidance to avoid spiritual pitfalls.
- **Impact of Personal Life on Ministry:** The personal lives of spiritual leaders, such as their marital relationships and how they handle personal challenges, significantly affect their public ministry and the spiritual health of their followers.
- **Preparation for Spiritual Warfare:** Those who carry significant spiritual mantles must be prepared for increased spiritual warfare, learning from how past leaders handled opposition and personal trials.

Conclusion

The principle of following as one is followed by Christ is pivotal not just in building personal faith but in sustaining the health and growth of the broader Christian community. This chapter outlines a framework for effective discipleship, emphasizing the need for vigilance, wisdom, and a deep commitment to the teachings of Jesus. It encourages believers to actively seek and maintain godly mentorship while being mindful of the inherent responsibilities and potential dangers it entails.

CHAPTER 18

CASE IN POINT: WILLIAM BRANHAM

Bible Verse

"Follow my example, as I follow the example of Christ." - 1 Corinthians 11:1

Introduction

This chapter examines the life and ministry of William Branham, highlighting both his profound impact on the charismatic movement and the cautionary lessons his story provides about the dangers of deviating from one's divine calling.

Word of Wisdom

"You have to know how to follow someone as that person follows the Lord."
- Roberts Liardon

Summary of Mantles Past and Present

Main Theme

Exploring the life of William Branham, this chapter serves as a stark reminder of the need for discernment in spiritual leadership, illustrating how even the most gifted individuals can falter if they step outside their God-given roles.

Key Points

- William Branham was known for his extraordinary prophetic and healing ministry.
- Branham's early ministry was marked by dramatic signs and wonders.
- Despite his spiritual gifts, Branham later deviated into erroneous teachings.
- His departure from his primary calling led to significant personal and doctrinal errors.
- Branham's life is both an inspiration and a warning to those in spiritual leadership.

Key Themes

- **The Impact of Spiritual Gifts:**
  Branham's ministry demonstrated the powerful impact of spiritual gifts, attracting large crowds and leading many to faith through signs and wonders. His initial adherence to his calling showcases the potential of a ministry aligned with God's will.
- **The Danger of Role Confusion:**
  Branham's later years exemplify the danger

of assuming roles not ordained by God. His attempt to shift from a prophetic to a teaching ministry led to doctrinal errors and diminished the effectiveness of his work.

- **The Importance of Spiritual Accountability:** Branham's story underscores the necessity for leaders to remain accountable and receptive to correction. Isolation and lack of accountability can lead to significant spiritual missteps.
- **Consequences of Deviating from God's Call:** Branham's deviation from his calling resulted in personal tragedy and a tarnished legacy, emphasizing the critical importance of staying true to one's divine purpose.
- **Learning from Historical Figures in Ministry:** Branham's life teaches that while it is important to respect and learn from past leaders, discernment is crucial. It is essential to recognize their failures and successes to navigate one's own spiritual journey wisely.

Conclusion

William Branham's ministry offers valuable lessons on the power and peril of spiritual leadership. While his early years were marked by divine favor and miraculous works, his later departure from God's specific calling serves as a cautionary tale. This chapter calls for a balanced view of spiritual heritage, advocating for admiration of the gifts while also recognizing the critical need for doctrinal soundness and personal humility.

CHAPTER 19

PASSING ON A MANTLE: NAVIGATING THE TRANSITION

Bible Verse

2 Kings 2:9 - "And it came to pass, when they were gone over, that Elijah said unto Elisha, Ask what I shall do for thee, before I be taken away from thee. And Elisha said, I pray thee, let a double portion of thy spirit be upon me."

Introduction

This chapter explores the biblical and historical concept of mantles—spiritual legacies and assignments passed from one generation to another. It emphasizes the importance of preparing and qualifying for these roles, highlighting both successful and failed transitions in biblical history.

Word of Wisdom

"God doesn't want His mantles stuck

in the graves of the last generation!"
Roberts Liardon

Main Theme

The transfer of spiritual mantles requires not only divine selection but also human readiness and righteousness. The chapter discusses how personal failure to adhere to God's standards can lead to dormant mantles and unfulfilled destinies.

Key Points

• Spiritual mantles are meant to be passed down through generations but can remain unclaimed due to lack of qualified successors.

• Gehazi's failure to inherit Elisha's mantle exemplifies the consequences of personal greed and moral failure.

• Mantles can lie dormant when individuals called to carry them do not meet the spiritual or moral requirements.

• Successful transmission of a mantle depends as much on the receiver's preparedness as on the giver's intention.

• The story of Samuel and his sons illustrates that even righteous leaders can fail in passing on their legacy if they do not address familial and personal shortcomings.

Key Themes

- **Dormant Mantles and Missed Opportunities:** Many spiritual mantles lie unclaimed not due to a lack of power or divine will but because of the potential successors' failure to align with God's requirements. The mantle remains powerful and capable of miraculous acts, as illustrated by the story of Elisha's bones reviving a dead man.
- **Gehazi's Disqualification:** Gehazi's failure underscores a crucial lesson that personal integrity and adherence to prophetic discipline are essential for inheriting spiritual responsibilities. His greed and deceit not only cost him the mantle but also led to his and his descendants' suffering.
- **The Role of Spiritual Parenthood:** The chapter emphasizes the importance of spiritual leaders acting as mentors, actively engaging in addressing and correcting the character flaws of their successors, much like a parent with a child.
- **Legacy of Righteousness:** The life of Samuel demonstrates how a righteous life can ensure the continuation of a spiritual mantle, whereas his failure with his sons showcases the impact of neglecting familial discipline.
- **Importance of Divine Approval:** The ultimate transfer of a mantle is depicted as a divine act requiring God's approval, not just human actions or desires. The right successor must be both called by God and

prepared to act in accordance with His will.

Conclusion

Passing on a mantle is a divine process intertwined with human responsibility. It requires more than being in the right place at the right time; it demands a life lived in line with God's statutes and a heart fully committed to His service. Leaders must nurture their successors, ensuring they are spiritually, morally, and emotionally equipped to handle the responsibilities they are to inherit.

CHAPTER 20

IT'S TIME!

Bible Verse

Ephesians 4:12-13 - "To equip his people for works of service, so that the body of Christ may be built up until we all reach unity in the faith and in the knowledge of the Son of God and become mature, attaining to the whole measure of the fullness of Christ."

Introduction

This concluding chapter emphasizes the urgency and importance of recognizing and embracing the spiritual mantles given by God under both Old and New Covenants. It calls for the rightful succession and deployment of these mantles to advance God's Kingdom on earth.

Word of Wisdom

"No person is given the power to determine how the mantles that Heaven bestows are distributed." Roberts Liardon

SUMMARY OF MANTLES PAST AND PRESENT

Main Theme

The chapter discusses the mantle of Christ as the primary mantle under the New Covenant, supplemented by specific mantle assignments that continue to be crucial in achieving God's purposes through His Church.

Key Points

- The mantle of Christ is the dominant spiritual inheritance for all believers, enhancing the Old Covenant's Elijah-Elisha mantle.

- Spiritual mantles can also rest on a collective, such as a church, rather than solely on individuals.

- The transfer of these mantles must prioritize God's intentions and not human ambitions.

- Believers should respect and support those carrying mantles without envy or competition.

- Understanding and correctly handling spiritual mantles is crucial for the Church's effectiveness in the last days.

Key Themes

- **Comprehensive Coverage of Mantles:**
  The mantle of Christ envelops every believer, offering the highest spiritual authority and power available. Additional specific mantles still operate to address particular Kingdom assignments,

emphasizing that no single mantle replaces another but rather they work in complement.

- **Collective vs. Individual Mantles:** Some mantles are bestowed upon entire congregations or communities to empower collective action for a divine purpose, demonstrating that the scope of God's work often extends beyond individual capacities.
- **Proper Succession of Mantles:** The correct transfer of spiritual mantles is critical and requires divine approval, rather than being a mere human decision. This process ensures that the power and responsibilities of these mantles are bestowed upon those truly prepared by God.
- **Role of Believers in Supporting Mantle Carriers:** Believers who are not mantle carriers play a vital role by supporting and upholding those who are, recognizing the significance of these gifts without falling into jealousy or rivalry.
- **Urgency in Spiritual Preparedness and Succession:** In these "last days," the urgency for the Church to understand and engage with spiritual mantles correctly is paramount for fulfilling God's ultimate plan on earth.

Conclusion

"It's Time!" serves as a rallying cry for the Church to embrace and action the responsibilities of spiritual mantles. As God prepares to enact a new phase in His divine plan, the Church must be ready to accept, support, and implement the spiritual legacies that have been ordained for this time, ensuring that each mantle is carried with integrity and purpose. This preparation and active participation will enable the Church to rise to its calling and manifest God's power and love on earth effectively.

Harrison House is a Spirit-filled, Word of Faith Christian publisher dedicated to spreading the message of faith, hope, and love through our wide range of inspiring publications. Committed to the messages that highlight the power of the Word and Spirit, we provide books, devotionals, and study guides that empower believers to live victorious, faith-filled lives.

Our resources are designed to help readers grow spiritually, strengthen their faith, and experience the transformative power of God's Word. Harrison House is passionate about equipping Christians with the tools they need to fulfill their divine purpose and impact the world for Christ.